Shadows of my Higher Self

Daija Ray

BookLeaf
Publishing

Presentation by *BookLeaf Publishing*

Web: www.bookleafpub.com

E-mail: info@bookleafpub.com

ISBN: 9789357446105

First edition 2023

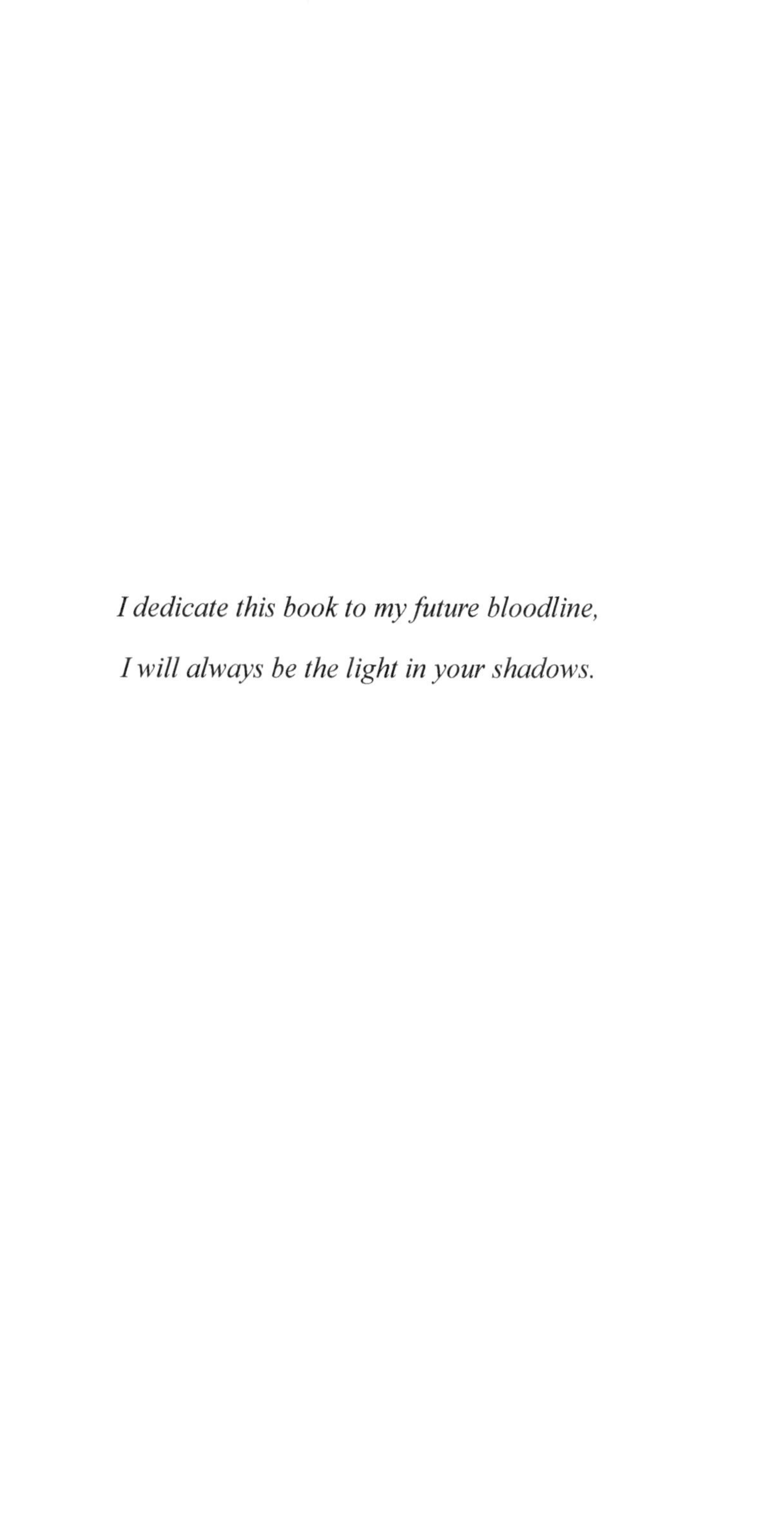

I dedicate this book to my future bloodline,

I will always be the light in your shadows.

ACKNOWLEDGEMENT

I want to send gratitude to all the genuine souls I've met along the way.
Thank you for the role you've played in the elevation

One love

PREFACE

This publication is quite personal to me.

I have long had a passion for creating in almost any form. The magic behind making something from nothing is absolutely captivating. It was years later when I realized that my passion had been recycled throughout generations. I watched the family around me create things at whim, and their souls would spark. Whether it was creating song, art, or stories my bloodline was blessed with creation.

However, it seemed a generational curse limited our very strength.

Things like publication rights or exposure have kept real creators in cages. This was personal because I want to relate to creators of all ages.

Some people might not want to hear it but others need you to say it

Even if no one sees the magic

doesn't mean you stop creating.

Born in the Dark

Right side up, lights out, no love in the air
Take it from me
A baby who was born in the same form they
were conceived
A fucking tragedy
The most connection I've had with my parents is
when the sperm met the egg
And briefly, we were considered a family
But please tell me
since when does mother hen drop her egg off
and leave it?
And what's the sense in planting seeds
with no urge to reap it

A cold shoulder to your newborn daughter
And when the cradle tipped over
You never caught her
What growth is expected of the abandoned?
I'm suppose to take on how much damage?
Before you take responsibility for the rebellion
That you had a hand in

The crack in the rose colored glass

Your tinted lenses
have adapted
to the darkness
Your sight is stronger
 than the shadows
They don't have to see the vision
Your assignment involves the unseen

The Heir of reparations

I can't stop until I feel the crack
In the foundation of generational curses
Until my bloodline receives its spiritual
reparations;
My Sons and Daughters can can know their
True heritage
They can claim the kingdoms built on the backs
of those who looked like them.

Invisible

I wish you could see me
I wish you had the capacity to miss me
I wish my love for you could fit into your
schedule

But I still hope you're happy
I hope you're thinking of me when I'm excluded

Spirit animal

Walking the path
Proud and Alone
Still trying to find that place to call
Home
The wolf does not fear darkness or isolation
She is terrified of conformity
 Earth's biggest temptation
The Lion & Tiger are among the most popular
But the Wolf would never perform in the Circus
For the pleasure of
one's ocular
She howls to the shadows
And dances with the moon
You'll fall in love with the girl
With the wolf tattoo
Just by watching how she moves

Our zone

Your energy gives me a rush of adrenaline
Being near you enhances my senses
I would recognize you in every dimension

I acknowledge your power, all ways

The balance

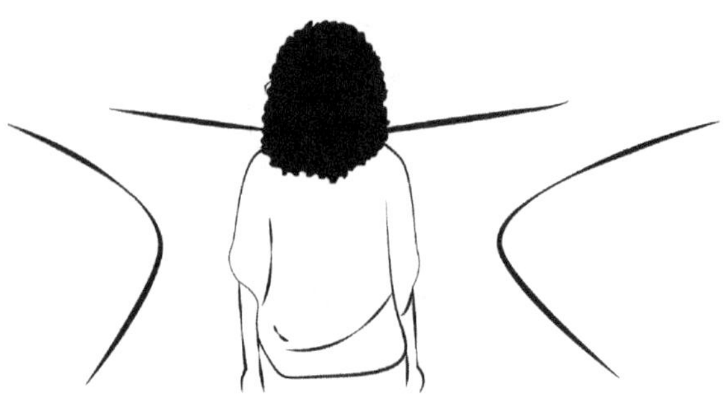

The stars are the silver lining in my darkness
In my nightmares, I find my wildest dreams

The scraps of pain that refused to heal
I turned into passion
I was blessed with beauty and rage
A true spiritual assassin

Chaos

To create in the chaos
Is to respect the fire
And utilize its intensity

-Burn shit down with that same fire
When necessary

Lost Kid

her brain lapses
and she forgets what's happened
so i gotta explain it
brain gotta reload it
relive it, replay it
the trauma that day
caused a shock to my system
heart ain't know what had hit it

physically, brought me to my knees
mentally, fucked me up
spiritually, rocked my foundation
   nobody picked me up

These are the people that raised me
no matter what, always forgave me

you were my light in the dark
the spark in my heart
my excuse & my reason,
my Sun in every season

Everything with intention

At some point, you have to
Trust in your own magic
The intention is part of
The spell

Power of the tongue

The tides of the Ocean flow off my tongue
I speak a divine language
But understand that things unsaid
Hold just as much power
My silence speaks volumes
If you listen closely

Freedom

Freedom is a birthright

Don't let anyone define it for you
You'll know what it feels like
For the good of all
& with harm to none

Alchemy

I know myself enough to know
The entire universe will bend to my will
I am the Alchemist
I have reign over my reality

-I may rebrand myself as I please
The essence of Alchemy

444

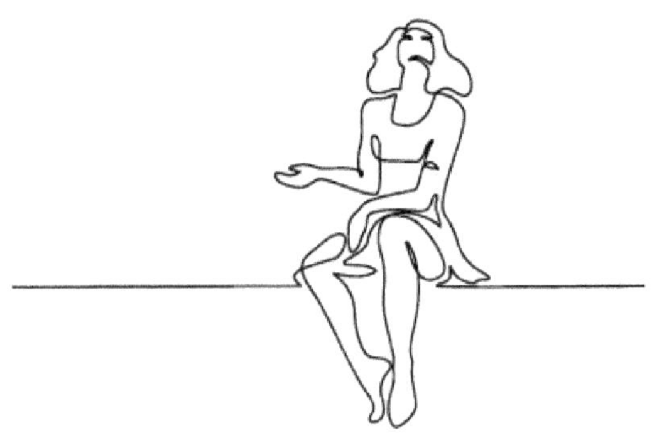

The guidance feels like bliss
In moments of heavy fog
I feel you in spaces you otherwise
Wouldn't be able to come along
There are parts of me that struggle with
The physical loss
But my guardian angels will forever
Speak life through me

Through the whispers of the wind
I can feel the presence of your wings

Learn and Return

We are here to live and learn
What do you learn from
 being afraid to live?
what the universe has to offer
Is more valuable than any earthly gain
Return with self knowledge
Or you'll have to learn the lessons again

Inner strength

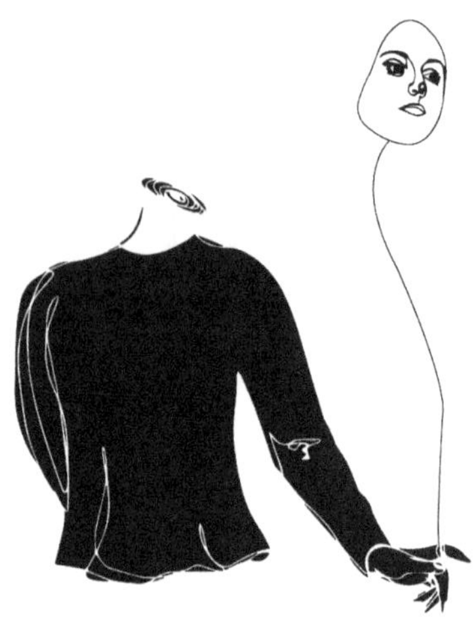

What a waste to have such a fire in you
And not raise a little hell

How dare you be given the gift of strength
And still choose to fail
You've already swallowed the fire
And now you're scared of a little rain

-get a grip, respectfully

Open to receive

You know
the greatness
that you're
destined for

Now let life give it to you.

Thin line between beauty and pain

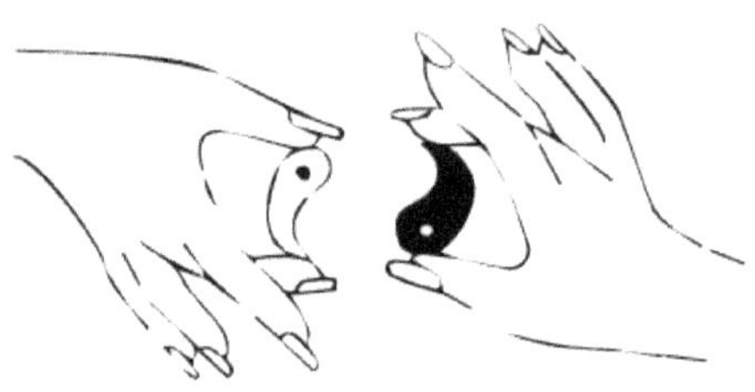

All my broken pieces
will one day
fit into the most beautiful vase
each shard
tells its own story
reflections of
all the layers I've shed
glued together with my
Higher purpose
displaying what I thought
was damage
as a powerful statement

The Cosmos

Wanderer by nature
who steps in divine timing
who flows like the waters
somehow always in Alignment
A spiritual free agent
completing a cosmic assignment

No fear

Don't be afraid to
harness the thunder
And let the Earth quake
In your honor

One Love

With Respect
to those who taught us our ways
with Love
for those who held us on the bad days
with Gratitude
All Ways